# ENDORSEMEN

MW01265483

When we hurt, it is good when those around us acknowledge our struggle. Jeff Jenkins' book *Beyond the Valley of Death*, however, takes us well past acknowledgement into the areas of the understanding and empathy for which our soul yearns when we suffer. Laura Jenkins was a monogenes ("one of a kind") woman. My wife and I knew her as an exceptional person and esteemed friend. Jeff's book is not just about her, but about his journey toward the other side of the valley of death since her promotion to glory. This book is a remarkable resource for those going through the grief journey, whatever the loss. Jeff's work represents many hours of contemplation, agony, tears, and loneliness in a positive way that helps others experience the light of hope and rebuilding. I wholeheartedly commend this book from the depths of his heart to yours.

*Dr. Ralph Gilmore*
*Retired Professor*
*Freed-Hardeman University*


It can feel almost impossible to live beyond the valley of death. After losing a child, parents, and a spouse, one of the kindest men I know writes about his experience. Jeff draws the reader into a compassionate and empathetic journey, sharing brief stories, helpful instruction, and tender understanding. You will feel as if Jeff has heard you and joined in the conversation with you. It is as if he says, "Me, too. Let's talk about it."

*David Shannon*
*President*
*Freed-Hardeman University*
*Henderson, Tennessee*


Jeff Jenkins is one of those rare treasures you sometimes have the fortune to discover. He loves God and people with a faithful passion that lifts all who know him to a better place and a better life. This book is another evidence of that.

With unflinching honesty, unflagging kindness, and unquenchable hope, Jeff allows us to walk with him and others in their journey of grief. He shares the resources that have helped and the experiences that have not.

In these words you find one who has not only walked through the valley of the shadow of death, but has done so with awareness, faith, and insight. This book will help you. It will do what Jeff has always done - it will lift you to a better place and a better life.

*Bill Watkins*
*Crieve Hall Church of Christ*
*Nashville, TN*


Jeff opens his heart to those whose hearts are broken and leads them to the heart of God. This book is a must for those in grief and those who help them.

*Paul Shero*
*Minister*
*Southgate Church of Christ*
*San Angelo, Texas*


"Life breaks everyone, and afterwards some are strong in the broken places"—Ernest Hemingway

My friend Jeff Jenkins embodies these words. He has trusted in the Lord all his life, and when he suffered a loss too painful to describe, the Lord he trusts has made him even stronger in the broken places. Jeff's faith has been tested in the fire. Let his words of wisdom and encouragement strengthen you.

*Chuck Monan*
*Minister*
*Pinnacle Church of Christ*
*Little Rock, Arkansas*


This brief book beautifully deals with trust in the midst of tears. Written by a grieving heart to those who are grieving or will grieve, Jeff writes with the God-centeredness, Bible-saturated and soul caring concern that many of us have come to treasure in him. Jeff is a preacher who has touched people's hearts for years wherever he has labored. In this book, we find out why - for we see the precious heart of Jesus in Jeff.

Thank you so much for writing of your experience.

*Mike Vestal*
*Minister, Westside Church of Christ*
*Midland TX*


"I just don't know what to say." Everyone who cares deeply has been frustrated by not knowing what words to speak to someone who has recently experienced profound loss. Everything we can think of sounds insufficient or perhaps even hurtful. In *Beyond the Valley of Death*, Jeff Jenkins offers us a resource for such moments. His very honest reflection on his own journey with grief may well be the gift that our grieving friends most need from us. I can imagine handing it to people and saying, "I am so sorry for what you are going through. I don't have anything to offer today except to say that I love you and to give you this book by Jeff Jenkins. When you are ready to read something about navigating this season in your life, I think you will find that my friend Jeff is

a very kind, gentle, thoughtful, genuine, and helpful companion through the valley of grief. You can trust him to be a faithful friend and brother."
*Bruce McLarty*
*Preacher*
*Cookeville, Tennessee*


Our dear friend, Jeff Jenkins, reveals his very personal insights regarding grief and loss relating to his precious Laura's death. Jeff has had to cross the chasm of grief more than once and he peels back the layers of grief as He takes this journey through the valley of grief. He gives us poignant reminders of why we grieve in life, that is, because we love! His book is also filled with hope, with realism, and with a promise that God and His Word will strengthen us as we travel our own grief journey. Everyone who reads this book will be both comforted and better equipped to comfort others. We wholeheartedly recommend this book as a valuable resource when dealing with losses in your life.
*Ron and Don Williams*
*RonDon Books*


*Beyond the Valley of Death* is more than a book on grieving. It's a window into the heart of a man of God who is still raw with emotion but rapt in hope. Jeff Jenkins comes from the perspective of both mourner and minister as he affirms one's lamenting while lovingly pointing the reader back to the God who grieves with us. This is not a theological treatise on death and dying. Rather, this is a personal and practical guide for getting through what you're going through. I am confident that anyone walking through the valley of death will derive comfort and inspiration from the thoughts expressed by a man who is walking the same path.

*Chris McCurley*
*Minister*
*Oldham Lane Church of Christ*
*Abilene, Texas*


One of the sad realities in life is that at some point everyone will deal with the loss of someone they dearly love. For many, the grief associated with that loss is often overwhelming and all-consuming. In his book, *Beyond the Valley of Death*, Jeff Jenkins shares his personal experience of loss and gives very practical advice on handling the sorrow that follows. Through many passages of Scripture, Jeff offers comfort, peace, and reassurance that God is always present. This wonderful book will be a tremendous benefit to those who have recently suffered the loss of a loved one, as well as anyone seeking to better understand the challenges and strategies for dealing with grief.

*Keith Harris*
*Minister*
*Windsong Church of Christ*
*Little Rock, Arkansas*


Many are hurting and need the sage, practical, and loving help this book provides. Jeff's approach is reassuring, practical, and full of grace and truth. Like our Lord, Jeff is a man "acquainted with grief." He hasn't just read about grief; he's living it. His book offers a Bible-centered, God-honoring and compassionate approach to coping with what he says is "the most challenging season of life." If you have lost a spouse (or any loved one) please read this book! If you won't read it for yourself, then read it so that you can recommend it to others. It will make an enormous, positive difference in the lives of those who are hurting. It made a huge difference in mine. Thank you, Jeff!

*John W. Moore*
*Bible Passages*

# BEYOND THE
# VALLEY OF DEATH

# BEYOND THE VALLEY OF DEATH

*Comforting Thoughts*
*When I've Lost My Spouse*

JEFF A. JENKINS

Cover Design: Boo & Amanda Scott
Interior Layout: Joey Sparks

# WITH DEEP GRATITUDE

The list of people who should be thanked for their love, encouragement, and friendship, especially during the past few years of my life, is a mile long. If your name should deserve mention here and you do not see it, please know that I am deeply grateful for you, and please forgive me.

My children and grandchildren have been the greatest blessing in my life since the passing of our Lolli. It isn't fair that children should lose their mother at a relatively young age. Through their own grief, Amanda and Jeremy have comforted, cared for, and looked after their dad while still navigating their life without their mom. Evie, Ever, and Forest are too young to realize how much joy and peace they bring to my life every day! I pray that when they can understand the full extent of their loss, they will know how thankful Pops is for the joy they bring.

Our Lewisville Church Family has made this journey with us from the beginning of Laura's final bout with cancer, and they have faithfully stood beside me in my grief. Our shepherds have prayed with me, cried with me, walked with me, and made it possible for me to have the time I need. I will forever be indebted to this wonderful family of God's people. I love you all dearly.

My life is blessed every day to be able to work closely with my brother, Dale. He keeps me dreaming, growing, and working for the Lord. He encourages me daily. He drives me to keep going. I am thankful that I am blessed to work with him to encourage preachers through TJI and pray that we will be able to do so for many years to come.

There are four preachers (actually, there are hundreds, but particularly four), along with their spouses who have been our dearest friends on earth for many years. They came while Laura was ill. They interrupted their very busy schedules to come hold our hands, to pray with us, to make the journey with us. They canceled appointments to be here for our family when we remembered Laura's life. They continue to this day to check on me, to come see me, and to "be there" for me, whenever I need them. Thank you doesn't begin to do justice to how I feel toward Steve & Keitha, Ralph & Joyce, Paul & Patsy, and Bill & Bev. I love you all forever.

I am thankful to Christians around the world who have brought comfort to our family and who continually reach out to us regularly.

A special thanks to my fellow travelers in this special journey of grief. Thank you for your example. Thank you for your faithfulness to the Lord. Thank you for understanding better than anyone else can what the loss of your spouse does to your life.

Thanks to our friend, Joey Sparks for being the best editor, designer, formatter, and whatever else is needed. There is no way we could do what we do without you.

Thanks to Boo and Amanda for helping me design the cover of this book. It is perfect and exactly what we need.

Thanks to my friend, Dale Hubbert for challenging me to present a lesson about Losing a Spouse. It was not an easy lesson, but I'm not sure anyone would be reading these words if you had not called.

Thank you to my Kemo Sabe, Steve, for writing the foreword for this book, for your words of comfort at Laura's funeral, for traveling around the world with me, for a thousand meals, for calling me nearly every day to check on me, and for everything else. I love you, my brother. I'll meet you at noon!

# FOREWORD

In the late 1990's it was my pleasure to meet this young Alabama preacher, Jeff Jenkins. He was preaching in Oklahoma City, Oklahoma, and I was about 15 miles away as the crow flies, in North Edmond, Oklahoma. During the summer months on Wednesday evenings, it was a congregational tradition to invite various speakers to preach on an assigned theme and topic. One of my guests was Jeff Jenkins. It was there that I met Jeff and Laura Jenkins. You see, you just could not say Jeff Jenkins without including his sweet wife Laura in the sentence. If you knew Laura Colley Jenkins, it was obvious she was the sweet one. Jeff has a magnetism that grows on every person he meets.

The relationship between me and Jeff grew from that first Summer Series to this very day. As I write this foreword, he and I have just completed speaking together at an Elders workshop in Arkansas. Laura is still fresh on my mind as we talked about her many times over the ten hours Jeff and I spent together in the car. We laughed a lot, and got quiet for a few "odd times of silence" of pure reflection. That is what friends do. Sometimes you speak and most of the time you just listen.

Jeff lost his precious Laura two years ago. In many ways, it is like yesterday and then in some ways it seems like decades. There is still a huge hole in our lives. My wife, Keitha, and

Laura texted often and more often as the end was in sight for this sweet friend and sister on this earth.

Jeff, Laura, Keitha and I have been many places over the years together and we cherish each of those moments. We loved taking our sweethearts for Valentine Dinners in the Dallas area. On the Appian Way in Greece, we all stood on the road and placed our feet where we thought Paul may have stepped 2000 plus years ago. We paused and took a cell phone picture. I still have that picture and will treasure it and that memory for the rest of my life. Those shoes represent a favorite scripture of mine, Romans 10:15: "And how shall they preach, except they be sent? as it is written, how beautiful are the feet of them that preach the gospel of peace, and bring glad tidings of good things!"

Most preachers know being a preacher and doing what we do is in large part because of our wives. They help us daily. They give freely to "one and all" and help along the way. Laura was a wonderful, godly woman. She was a wonderful wife to Jeff, mother and grandmother. She was a confidant, a friend, and an encouragement to all she encountered throughout the years.

Jeff, I miss your sweet Laura. This book will be a wonderful encouragement to all who read it. Jeff's own words will pull you in. It will give you a little insight to the life of Laura. If you did not know Laura—you missed out. However, if you know Jeff, you will see part of Laura in him. Laura had beautiful feet long before she met Jeff at Freed Hardeman University. She did not preach from the pulpit as Jeff did and still does, but she let her life be a living sermon every day. I loved my sister in Christ, Laura Jenkins, and I want to see her again someday. Her life makes me want to go to heaven.

Jeff, thanks for being my friend. I love you. Let's do lunch together soon and I will always remember your sweet Laura.

*Stephen A. Bailey*
*Waxahachie, TX*

# A JOURNEY THROUGH THE VALLEY:
## *From the Valley of Death...To The Mountaintop of Life*

When the sweet singer of Israel wrote, "Even though I walk through the valley of the shadow of death, I fear no evil, for You are with me; Your rod and Your staff, they comfort me," (Psalm 23:4), he was likely referencing the comfort he received from God even as he felt he was near death.

However, any child of God, who has walked down into death's valley with someone who means more to them than life itself, senses the peace from God that passes all understanding.

In addition to the numerous times, I have spent time with families dealing with the death of a loved one for more than forty years in ministry, I have personally experienced this dark shadow at four specific moments in my adult life. The first encounter came when my wife and I buried our infant son, next when we lost my Mom, then when we lost my Dad. And the most recent, as well as most difficult time, lasted nearly two years in the valley of the shadow of death with my sweet wife.

Each of these seasons had their own special challenges, but none more difficult than the passing of my Laura. My sweet wife's battle with cancer began when she was in her early thirties. She went into remission, but it returned ten years later. Once again, the cancer seemed to be under control for about twelve more years, before it returned. The third time lasted nearly two years, and it was a difficult, constant battle that she bravely fought. The last time was just too much for her to overcome.

Many who will read these thoughts are in the valley now. Others have recently spent time watching the dearest person on earth to them pass through the valley of the shadow of death. And although others have gone through that dark valley many years ago, they may still have difficulty navigating life.

A couple of the lessons all of us learn who have traversed this valley or who have attempted to provide counsel for others is that no two journeys are the same. We have learned as well that we will be more helpful to one another, when we realize that what works for one person cannot serve as a uniform answer for everyone.

Losing your spouse will turn your world upside down, whether the loss is a sudden passing or after a long period of illness. You go to bed married. You wake up single, alone, confused, heartbroken, and grieving. As these intense emotions rush over you, your lifestyle changes forever. In addition to this new reality, there are numerous practical matters that result due to the death of your spouse that you may have to deal with or think about.

Overcoming such a big loss is no small task, but it helps to be aware of your process, symptoms, and reactions. Are they normal, expected grief? Or have you developed a mental health condition?

In the meantime, may I offer a few suggestions, some general, some more specific, that have been helpful for me and others. Please understand that I do not in any stretch of the imagination believe I've figured this out. My journey is still relatively new, and like many of you, I continue to search for ways to handle the pain of loss. I would sincerely love to hear from others who have endured time in the valley who would be willing to share what has been most helpful for them. *See my contact information in the resource section of this book.

# NO RIGHT WAY

## *There is no "right" way to feel after losing your spouse.*

So many variables contribute to your reaction, including how long and happy your marriage was, how your spouse died, how old your children are (if you have them), and how dependent you were on one another.

You may feel guilty for being the one who is still alive or relieved that your spouse is no longer suffering. You might even feel angry at your spouse for leaving you. You may cry a lot, or you may not. How you grieve is unique to you. You may find yourself in a state of shock, or depending on the circumstances, in denial. You may feel numb, anxious, and brokenhearted. You will feel overwhelmed and anxious about many immediate decisions as well as future concerns. Through the course of time, the grief can become less intense and with much prayer and help from others, you will begin to live in your "new normal."

It's not just the emotions. Grieving can affect our bodies as well. We can lose our appetite or have trouble sleeping. It is easier to say it than to do it. However, we need to try to take care of ourselves by eating well, exercising, and getting enough sleep.

## *Remember that you are not alone.*

One of the great promises in Scripture for all of God's people is that we do not have to walk this life alone. We read repeatedly that the God we serve is "present." You have to love these precious words from the wise King Solomon. "Trust in the Lord with all your heart and do not lean on your own understanding. In all your ways acknowledge Him, and He will make your paths straight" (Proverbs 3:5-6).

The promise that God gave to His wandering people is very applicable to those of us who are traveling in uncharted waters. "Be strong and courageous, do not be afraid or in dread of them, for the Lord your God is the One who is going with you. He will not desert you or abandon you" (Deuteronomy 31:6).

In addition to the promises from God that He will not leave us alone, Christians are blessed to be surrounded by an army of God's special people to hold us up. Since losing my wife, it has been beautiful and overwhelming to be strengthened by God's family from around the world. Calls, letters, cards, emails, messages, visits, kind acts from Christians literally around the world, have been one of the greatest blessings to my life.

My conviction is that when we are in what is without a doubt one of the most challenging seasons of life, we will be stronger by surrounding ourselves with people who love us, who care deeply for us, and with whom we enjoy spending time with from day to day. Included in this group would be our physical family. I do not know what I would have done during this time without the constant love and support of my two precious children and my three precious grandchildren, even as they dealt with their own grief. My physical family, my spiritual family, and my closest group of friends have been my champions and my heroes, during this difficult time.

## *Loneliness is one of life's biggest challenges.*

Because your spouse was such a major part of your daily life, their loss is usually felt more immediately and for a longer length of time. Regardless of the tenure of your marriage or relationship, this is the person you made long-term plans with and chose to spend your life with. You valued their unique qualities, their humor or charm, their intellect, kindness, or strength, and no one will ever take his or her place. As acute as your loss feels now, being alone doesn't mean a *lifetime* of loneliness. It may be tempting to isolate yourself at this time but reaching out to others for support is critical.

Studies suggest that a lack of social support after an unexpected loss is a key predictor of depression. For this reason, it is important to reach out to other people in your life for help. You may be inclined to turn inward, but you'll probably fare better if you seek support from family, friends, your church family (if you have one), or a counselor.

### *Be prepared for friends and family who may not know what to say or try to comfort you with cliches.*

You will be reminded that your spouse "is in a better place." Sometimes people will say, "Remember, she is always with you." I know they mean well, and there is a sense where we always carry our loved one in our hearts, but that phrase seems empty to me. If our loved one was with us, we wouldn't miss them so much.

When Laura and I lost our son many years ago, a dear, sweet sister came to visit. She meant well and we believed she loved us. Laura was in bed and this sweet lady came to "cheer her up." She stayed quite a long time and tried to make Laura laugh by telling many jokes. Laura was not in the mood to laugh, but she was so kind and receptive. There will be people who love you, who will say and do the wrong things.

Some are uncomfortable talking about death, but it doesn't mean they don't care. Others will avoid you for fear of saying the wrong thing or not knowing what to say. Again, it doesn't mean they don't love you or they don't care.

Close friends and at times, even family members will often ask questions that are difficult. They may intend to help, but unfortunately, they don't always know how challenging these questions are for someone who has lost their spouse.

Questions such as, "Are you doing this?" "What are you going to do about that?" "Have you thought about this particular matter?" "When are you going to…?" You may not be ready to deal with some of these questions yet, and there's nothing wrong with that.

If you can do so, and if you feel comfortable doing so, tell those close to you what you need (or don't need). If people avoid mentioning your spouse, for example, and you want to talk about them, let them know. Keep in mind that your friends and family are also grieving and may find it comforting to share memories of your spouse. There is nothing wrong with you saying, "I'm not ready to talk about that right now," or, "I need to talk about this now."

## *Recognize the value of God's precious Word.*

When the pandemic hit and changed our world, we began to think about ways we could help the church remain focused on the Word. We also wanted to find ways to encourage connection during a time that many would be isolated. We decided to offer a daily online Bible study. As of this writing, we have completed more than 500 days in a row (except for a handful of missed days). We spent more than five months in the Psalms. We spent about one month in Psalm 119 alone. With each lesson, I was reminded again of how valuable God's precious Word is to those of us who are walking through the valley of the shadow of death. The Word of God is written in part to bring us comfort, and when we study it prayerfully, indeed it does just that.

There are several excellent books available that can help you with outstanding practical advice for dealing with grief. I will mention some of them and how you can obtain them in the resource section at the end of this book.

However, in my heart I do not believe there is anything that has ever been written that will help any of us more than the Word of God, produced by our loving Father. "Blessed be the God and Father of our Lord Jesus Christ, the Father of mercies and God of all comfort, who comforts us in all our affliction so that we will be able to comfort those who are in any affliction with the comfort with which we ourselves are comforted by God. For just as the sufferings of Christ are ours in abundance, so also our comfort is abundant through Christ" (2 Corinthians 1:3-5).

## *Some things are just out of our control.*

One of the few things I don't enjoy about flying is the feeling of not having control. I'm a typical man. We like to "be in control" at work, in our family, of the TV remote, of our vehicles, of our pets, of our family, and even of our health. I'm in the air right now returning from visiting some dear friends. Our flight was delayed four times because of weather. We will arrive safely at DFW three hours later than our ETA!

We sat on the tarmac for about an hour. When I texted my family and friends to give them an update, they all said basically the same thing. They said, "Be safe and fly safe." My thought was, I don't have any control over whether I am safe on this flight. And, if I were the pilot, we certainly wouldn't be flying safe!!

But then something comforting happened. The pilot came on the loudspeaker and said, "We are going to take off folks, sit back and relax, don't worry about a thing. We're going to take good care of you!" And my entire feeling about the flight changed immediately.

Of course, you didn't want to let your spouse go. I know I didn't. However, I also didn't want to see her suffer any more. That was the most difficult part for me. Watching my sweet wife suffer. She didn't deserve it. If I said it once, I said it a thousand times. "I wish I can make your pain go away." "I wish I could take your pain and make it mine."

We prayed together every day that God would let her get well. But we both knew that we couldn't do anything about it, other than pray and follow the doctor's advice. We couldn't make her pain go away and we couldn't make her get well. We were not in control. If you trust God, I'm certain that you prayed for your spouse for weeks, months, or years, but she/he didn't recover. So, what do you do?

## *Let Go & Let God.*

Those words seem so trivial, trite, and at times even empty. Every time I hear someone say them, I cringe. My mind rushes to lead my mouth to comment. "That's easy for you to say. You haven't lost your spouse, your lifetime partner, that person who completes you and makes your life on earth bearable." I want to say, "Stop it, and shut up!" But of course, I don't.

If you are reading this book because you have lost your spouse, you understand. There are many times we want to lash out at those who speak words that ring hollow to us. But we don't.

They don't mean to hurt us. As a point of fact, they are trying to help us. People often don't know what to say, or even how to approach us. Particularly early on in our journey of grief.

Now that I've cleared the air on that, and I reconsider those words, in the big scheme of things, they may be helpful after all. What if that's really the best step we can take? What if we really should turn over everything to Him? After all, that's exactly what Jesus did.

Listen to this statement from one of the closest friends our Savior ever had: "For you have been called for this purpose, because Christ also suffered for you, leaving you an example, so that you would follow in His steps, He who committed no sin, nor was any deceit found in His mouth; and while being abusively insulted, He did not insult in return; while suffering, He did not threaten, but kept entrusting Himself to Him who judges righteously" (1 Peter 2:21-23).

While they were beating our Savior, He turned it over to His Father. While they were mocking Him, He turned it over to His Father. While they were ridiculing Him, jeering, and laughing at Him, He kept turning it all over to God. He literally, "Let go and let God." I know, it doesn't seem that easy, and my guess is, it wasn't easy for Him either. Yet rather than lashing out at others and make statements that we may regret later, maybe, just maybe, we should try to let go and let God.

## *Recall the importance of worship.*

Long before I began my personal journey through this dark valley, it seemed astounding to me to see how many Christians would turn away from worshiping God when they were encountering pain in their lives. After years of attempting to assist others and enduring various seasons of pain in my own life, that astonishment has only increased.

It is not my intent to be insensitive in any way, but anyone who believes it is a good choice to stay away from the worship of God when they are struggling with life, is sadly mistaken. We do not need less of God when we are hurting, we need more of Him!

When the man after God's heart believed that his child had died, he enquired of his servants, "Is the child dead?" When they responded that the boy had died, Samuel records the Kings response: "So, David got up from the ground, washed, anointed himself, and changed his clothes; and he went into the house of the Lord and worshiped" (2 Samuel 12:20). If you have endured the loss of the dearest on earth to you, I would plead with you not to stay away from worship, but rather respond in the way that David did.

## Our Foundation Family

I attended another funeral the other day. Part of me wishes I would have kept up with the number of funerals I've preached and attended through the years. That's probably because I'm a preacher and I can't help it! You know, we have this "numbers thing." I hope we can all overcome the numbers thing. But that's a different book! It does seem like there are more of them to preach and attend these days. That's probably because I'm getting old.

This funeral was for the Mom of one of our Lewisville ladies. She was a wonderful, kind-hearted, sweet, faithful Christian. It was obvious that she made a tremendous impact for good in everything she did. The speaker talked about several families who were integral to her life. He talked about her physical "Family." She and her husband were married for sixty years! They raised two wonderful children and had a super family.

Next, he spoke of her Girl Scout "Family." This sweet sister helped many young girls during their days with the Girl Scouts. She was loved deeply by all of them, and she guided many of these young ladies during crucial moments in their lives.

The preacher talked next about her Lowe's "Family." He talked about how she had worked at the Lowes Store in her town since the day it opened. She counseled many of the employees who would seek her out for advice. She was often the first person who greeted you when you entered the store, and she loved her work.

Lastly, he spoke of her Church "Family." He talked about how she had been a faithful worker in the Church for many, many years. Then he said something I had never thought about. He said, "It was this 'Family,' her Church Family that served as the foundation for everything she did with all of her other families." He suggested that she would not have been able to do as much with her other families if she did not have her Church Family as the foundation. Her Church Family made all her other families better.

WOW! All of us have different types of families in our lives. When we lose the dearest person on earth to us, it is not during this season of our life that we should stay away from our Church Family. I pray that you have a loving, supportive Church Family to help you in this part of your journey. My prayer is that you will reach out to them and not try to make this journey alone. If you don't have a loving, supportive Church family, I would love to help you with this "foundation" Family.

## *Restart your life when you feel ready.*

As we said earlier, every person must handle grief in their own way. There is no set or required time for those who remain to move forward into a new normal. Of course, our life will never be the same as it was before. We should take the time we need to grieve, but after that time, we need to reengage ourselves in the service of the Lord.

There may come a time when we have to force ourselves to re-engage and become busy again. In my life, being busy has been a blessing. Trying to help others and encourage them has helped me not to become mired in my own grief. Years ago, I remember hearing someone say, "It is better to act your way into a feeling than it is to feel your way into an action." That may become appropriate in our lives when we are enduring loss.

How do I know when I'm ready? One way to help with this is to consider the different stages of grief. If we can determine where we are in our grief, we will better know when we are ready to journey into our new life.

# FIVE STAGES OF GRIEF

*On Grief and Grieving* is still the gold standard when it comes to books written by humans; co-authored by Elisabeth Kübler-Ross and David Kessler in 1969. Kessler writes, "The stages have evolved since their introduction and have been very misunderstood over the past four decades. They were never meant to help tuck messy emotions into neat packages. They are responses to loss that many people have, but there is not a typical response to loss as there is no typical loss."

## *Denial*

Denial is the first of the five stages of grief. It helps us to survive the loss. In this stage, the world becomes meaningless and overwhelming. Life makes no sense. We are in a state of shock and denial. We go numb. We wonder how we can go on, if we can go on, why we should go on. We try to find a way to simply get through each day. Denial and shock help us to cope and make survival possible. Denial helps us to pace our feelings of grief. There is a grace in denial. It is nature's way of letting in only as much as we can handle. As you accept the reality of the loss and start to ask yourself questions, you are unknowingly beginning the healing process. You are becoming stronger, and the denial is beginning to fade. But as you proceed, all the feelings you were denying begin to surface.

## Anger

Anger is a necessary stage of the healing process. Be willing to feel your anger, even though it may seem endless. The more you truly feel it, the more it will begin to dissipate and the more you will heal. There are many other emotions under the anger, and you will get to them in time, but anger is the emotion we are most used to managing. The truth is that anger has no limits. It can extend not only to your friends, the doctors, your family, yourself and your loved one who died, but also to God. You may ask, "Where is God in this?' Underneath anger is pain, your pain. It is natural to feel deserted and abandoned, but we live in a society that fears anger. Anger is strength and it can be an anchor, giving temporary structure to the nothingness of loss. At first grief feels like being lost at sea: no connection to anything. Then you get angry at someone, maybe a person who didn't attend the funeral, maybe a person who isn't around, maybe a person who is different now that your loved one has died. Suddenly you have a structure: your anger toward them. The anger becomes a bridge over the open sea, a connection from you to them. It is something to hold onto; and a connection made from the strength of anger feels better than nothing. We usually know more about suppressing anger than feeling it. The anger is just another indication of the intensity of your love.

## Bargaining

Before a loss, it seems like you will do anything if only your loved one would be spared. "Please God," you bargain, "I will never be angry at my wife again if you'll just let her live." After a loss, bargaining may take the form of a temporary truce. "What if I devote the rest of my life to helping others? Then can I wake up and realize this has all been a bad dream?" We become lost in a maze of "If only..." or "What if..." statements. We want life returned to what it was; we want our loved one restored. We want to go back in time: find the tumor sooner, recognize the illness more quickly, stop the accident from happening...if only, if only, if only. Guilt is often bargaining's companion. "If only" causes us to find fault in ourselves and what we "think" we could have done differently. We may even bargain with the pain. We will do anything not to feel the pain of this loss. We remain in the past, trying to negotiate our way out of the hurt. People often think of the stages as lasting weeks or months. They forget that the stages are responses to feelings that can last for minutes or hours as we flip in and out of one and then another. We do not enter and leave each individual stage in a linear fashion. We may feel one, then another and back again to the first one.

## *Depression*

After bargaining, our attention moves squarely into the present. Empty feelings present themselves, and grief enters our lives on a deeper level, deeper than we ever imagined. This depressive stage feels as though it will last forever. It's important to understand that this depression is not a sign of mental illness. It is the appropriate response to a great loss. We withdraw from life, left in a fog of intense sadness, wondering, perhaps, if there is any point in going on alone? Why go on at all? Depression after a loss is too often seen as unnatural: a state to be fixed, something to snap out of. The first question to ask yourself is whether the situation you're in is depressing. The loss of a loved one is a very depressing situation, and depression is a normal and appropriate response. To not experience depression after a loved one dies would be unusual. When a loss fully settles in your soul, the realization that your loved one didn't get better this time and is not coming back is understandably depressing. If grief is a process of healing, then depression is one of the many necessary steps along the way.

## *Acceptance*

Acceptance is often confused with the notion of being "all right" or "OK" with what has happened. This is not the case. Most people don't ever feel OK or all right about the loss of a loved one. This stage is about accepting the reality that our loved one is physically gone and recognizing that this new reality is the permanent reality. We will never like this reality or make it OK, but eventually we accept it. We learn to live with it. It is the new norm with which we must learn to live. We must try to live now in a world where our loved one is missing. In resisting this new norm, at first many people want to maintain life as it was before a loved one died.

In time, through bits and pieces of acceptance, however, we see that we cannot maintain the past intact. It has been forever changed and we must readjust. We must learn to reorganize roles, re-assign them to others or take them on ourselves. Finding acceptance may be just having more good days than bad ones. As we begin to live again and enjoy our life, we often feel that in doing so, we are betraying our loved one. We can never replace what has been lost, but we can make new connections, new meaningful relationships, new inter-dependencies. Instead of denying our feelings, we listen to our needs; we move, we change, we grow, we evolve. We may start to reach out to others and become involved in their lives. We invest in our friendships and in our relationship with ourselves. We begin to live again, but we cannot do so until we have given grief it's time.

Many people look for "closure" after a loss. Kessler argues that it's finding meaning beyond the stages of grief most of us are familiar with—denial, anger, bargaining, depression, and acceptance—that can transform grief into a more peaceful and hopeful experience.

In this book, Kessler gives readers a roadmap to remembering those who have died with more love than pain; he shows us how to move forward in a way that honors our loved ones. Kessler's insight is both professional and intensely personal. His journey with grief began when, as a child, he witnessed a mass shooting at the same time his mother was dying. For most of his life, Kessler taught physicians, nurses, counselors, police, and first responders about end of life, trauma, and grief, as well as leading talks and retreats for those experiencing grief. Despite his knowledge, his life was upended by the sudden death of his twenty-one-year-old son.

## *Finding Meaning*

How does this grief expert handle such a tragic loss? He knew he had to find a way through this unexpected, devastating loss, a way that would honor his son. That, ultimately, was the sixth state of grief—meaning. In *Finding Meaning*, Kessler shares the insights, collective wisdom, and powerful tools that will help those experiencing loss.

Isn't that what we all ultimately long to do? We want to honor our spouse by once again finding meaning and purpose in our lives. How we honor our spouse will look different for every person and it will change at various stages in life.

Some will find meaning and honor their spouse by re-marrying. Those who choose this path should never feel doing so says they have quit loving their spouse or even replaced the love they had for their spouse who has gone on to be with the Lord. Often, a widow and widower will meet and fall in love. They both under-stand the depth of love that one must have for a spouse. I have known many people who have honored their spouse who has gone on to be with the Lord and hon-ored their current spouse as well.

Others may find meaning and honor their spouse by dedicating their life to a cause. It could be some specific ministry in the life of the Church, working with some other organization, or traveling to places their spouse enjoyed seeing. My friend, Dean Miller has committed his life to encouraging Christians who have lost their spouse through *Widowhood Workshop*. If you can at-tend one of these workshops, your life will be richly blessed.

My sweet Laura loved preachers and preachers' wives. She particularly loved preachers' wives. I think we should be careful about saying words like, "never, always, and forever," regarding remarriage or remaining single, especially during the early stages of our grief journey. Having made that clear, at this point in my journey, my plan is to spend the rest of my life encouraging and working with preachers and their families. It will require extensive travel for longer periods of time. Because of that I don't believe I will remarry.

Every child of God can find meaning in life and honor their beloved spouse by making sure we follow their path to heaven. We can also honor them by trying to take as many people with us to heaven as possible.

## HEAVEN SEEMS SWEETER

All my life, I've thought about, studied about, written about, learned about, preached about, and longed for Heaven. But Heaven has never seemed sweeter than it does when we think about going to be with our loved ones who have gone before us.

As I bring these thoughts to a conclusion, I will confess to you that this has not been an easy book to write. By the time you have this book in your hands it will have been two years since my family and I buried our sweet Laura. After these two years, we/I still miss her every day. Some days, without any notice and for no apparent reason, a wave of grief engulfs me.

Since our journey beyond the valley of death began, I have spoken with more people who have lost a spouse than I could imagine. Some of these wonderful people have begun their journey even more recently than I began mine. Some lost their spouse many years ago and have spoken of how time seems to help, but the pain is still present.

A close friend related the following thoughts to me. Several years ago, in Japan an earthquake occurred that registered 9.0. Following the earthquake there was a tsunami that killed 18,000 people and caused disastrous meltdowns at a nuclear power plant. Ten years later Japan had spent more than 280 million dollars in recovery and rebuilding. "Even after ten years an 81-year-old man who lost a grandchild in the disaster said, 'The wounds of the heart remain.'"

As we move forward and rely on the strength of God and His people, the wounds may never leave our hearts. Perhaps the corners of those wounds can be softened, and we can use the help we have received to soften the blows to the heart of someone else.

We understand that our pain has a purpose. We see so much hurt in the lives of people we love and others we don't even know.

We are fellow strugglers in this life. We do well to encourage one another, support one another, and pray for one another. We need each other as we journey through life. We are reminded that our life has purpose, and we have a mission. Our purpose is to glorify God with everything we have and everything we are. Our mission is to share the message of Jesus with everyone we can and help one another make it to Heaven.

Yes, we weep because of our pain, and we long for the time when we can be with our Lord. However, until that time, we expend every ounce of our being to bring glory to Him and to encourage others who are hurting. We are deeply thankful for the love, support, prayers, and encouragement from so many. May God bless you today and every day as you seek to please Him.

If these words are helpful to you in any way, and if God is glorified, it will be a worthwhile effort. Please know that as you continue your journey that you will be in my prayers. Also, there are many others who walk with you, arm in arm who will be praying for you. May your life be enriched by the God of all comfort, "who comforts us in all our affliction, so that we may be able to comfort those who are in any affliction, with the comfort with which we ourselves are comforted by God." If I can be of help to you in any way, please feel free to reach out to me.

# COMFORTING TEXT MESSAGES FROM THE GOD OF ALL COMFORT

### Revelation 21:4

He will wipe away every tear from their eyes, and death shall be no more, neither shall there be mourning, nor crying, nor pain anymore, for the former things have passed away.

### 1 Thessalonians 4:13-18

But we do not want you to be uninformed, brothers, about those who are asleep, that you may not grieve as others do who have no hope. For since we believe that Jesus died and rose again, even so, through Jesus, God will bring with him those who have fallen asleep. For this we declare to you by a word from the Lord, that we who are alive, who are left until the coming of the Lord, will not precede those who have fallen asleep. For the Lord himself will descend from heaven with a cry of command, with the voice of an archangel, and with the sound of the trumpet of God. And the dead in Christ will rise first. Then we who are alive, who are left, will be caught up together with them in the clouds to meet the Lord in the air, and so we will always be with the Lord. Therefore, comfort one another with these words.

### Romans 8:28
And we know that for those who love God all things work together for good, for those who are called according to his purpose.

### John 14:1-3
Let not your hearts be troubled. Believe in God; believe also in me. In my Father's house are many rooms. If it were not so, would I have told you that I go to prepare a place for you? And if I go and prepare a place for you, I will come again and will take you to myself, that where I am you may be also.

### Romans 14:8

For if we live, we live to the Lord, and if we die, we die to the Lord. So then, whether we live or whether we die, we are the Lord's.

### Romans 6:23

For the wages of sin is death, but the free gift of God is eternal life in Christ Jesus our Lord.

### Psalm 23:1-6

The Lord is my shepherd; I shall not want. He makes me lie down in green pastures. He leads me beside still waters. He restores my soul. He leads me in paths of righteousness for his name's sake. Even though I walk through the valley of the shadow of death, I will fear no evil, for you are with me; your rod and your staff, they comfort me. You prepare a table before me in the presence of my enemies; you anoint my head with oil; my cup overflows. Surely goodness and mercy shall follow me all the days of my life, and I shall dwell in the house of the LORD forever.

*Hebrews 13:5*
Keep your life free from love of money, and be content with what you have, for he has said, "I will never leave you nor forsake you."

*Luke 23:43*
And he said to him, "Truly, I say to you, today you will be with me in Paradise."

*1 Chronicles 16:11*
Seek the Lord and his strength; seek his presence continually!

*Philippians 1:21*
For to me to live is Christ, and to die is gain.

*2 Corinthians 5:8*
Yes, we are of good courage, and we would rather be away from the body and at home with the Lord.

*1 Corinthians 15:51-57*
Behold! I tell you a mystery. We shall not all sleep, but we shall all be changed, in a moment, in the twinkling of an eye, at the last trumpet. For the trumpet will sound, and the dead will be raised imperishable, and we shall be changed. For this perishable body must put on the imperishable, and this mortal body must put on immortality. When the perishable puts on the imperishable, and the mortal puts on immortality, then shall come to pass the saying that is written: "Death is swallowed up in victory." "O death, where is your victory? O death, where is your sting?" The sting of death is sin, and the power of sin is the law. But thanks be to God, who gives us the victory through our Lord Jesus Christ. Therefore, my beloved brothers, be steadfast, immov-

able, always abounding in the work of the Lord, knowing that in the Lord your labor is not in vain.

*1 Corinthians 15:26*
The last enemy to be destroyed is death.

*Ecclesiastes 12:7*
And the dust returns to the earth as it was, and the spirit returns to God who gave it.

*Psalm 116:15*
Precious in the sight of the Lord is the death of his saints.

*Revelation 20:6*
Blessed and holy is the one who shares in the first resurrection! Over such the second death has no power, but they will be priests of God and of Christ, and they will reign with him for a thousand years.

*Hebrews 9:27*

And just as it is appointed for man to die once, and after that comes judgment.

*Philippians 1:23*

I am hard pressed between the two. My desire is to depart and be with Christ, for that is far better.

*2 Corinthians 1:3-4*

Blessed be the God and Father of our Lord Jesus Christ, the Father of mercies and God of all comfort, who comforts us in all our affliction, so that we may be able to comfort those who are in any affliction, with the comfort with which we ourselves are comforted by God.

*John 11:25*

Jesus said to her, "I am the resurrection and the life. Whoever believes in me, though he dies, yet shall he live."

*John 11:32-36*
Now when Mary came to where Jesus was and saw him, she fell at his feet, saying to him, "Lord, if you had been here, my brother would not have died." When Jesus saw her weeping, and the Jews who had come with her also weeping, he was deeply moved in his spirit and greatly troubled. And he said, "Where have you laid him?" They said to him, "Lord, come and see." Jesus wept. So the Jews said, "See how he loved him!"

*John 10:10*
The thief comes only to steal and kill and destroy. I came that they may have life and have it abundantly.

*John 5:24*
Truly, truly, I say to you, whoever hears my word and believes him who sent me has eternal life. He does not come into judgment but has passed from death to life.

*John 3:16-17*
For God so loved the world, that he gave his only Son, that whoever believes in him should not perish but have eternal life. For God did not send his Son into the world to condemn the world, but in order that the world might be saved through him.

*Philippians 4:13*
I can do all things through him who strengthens me.

# COMFORTING TEXTS MESSAGES FROM THE HEARTS OF SOME WHO HAVE LOST A SPOUSE

***From Barbara:***
1) Staying in the Word
2) Staying busy
3) Fellowship with my brethren especially those who have also lost mates.
4) Knowledge that God is constantly by my side
5) Comfort in knowledge that Glen is with the Father waiting for me
6) Strong body of Christians with solid leadership and preachers and teachers committed to proclaiming the truth.

***From Juanita***
The pain of grief is real-but so is the peace that comes from God. I have found through prayer, the study of God's Word, and the support of loved ones, I can find comfort and strength. I would say to others who face the loss of a spouse, God

will help you feel His Peace and His love; a peace that passes all understanding. Rely on God and others to help relieve the sorrow and provide you with support (Psalms 34:18 and Isaiah 41:10).

### *From Dean*

The first verse and chorus of "Heaven Will Surely Be Worth It All." For the past several years (during both caregiving & widowhood), in my darkest hours, I have orally quoted to myself those words. At my wife's memorial service (12/30/2013), I had a young man sing that song solo. I used to tell my daughters the only request I had for my funeral was for those gathered there to sing that song. The message of that song has often given me strength to breathe when I felt I couldn't and keep trying when I didn't feel like it.

### *From Elizabeth*

The things that are different regarding the absence of Joe are not having someone who understands the problems within a discussion about decisions, and second just not having someone to discuss the normal, even the weather. The quiet house was something I treasured but now without him it is too quiet.

I just cannot imagine ever being separated from Jesus or God. I am not saying that I am perfect because of course I am not, but just can't grapple with the idea of separating myself from HIM. It was the way I was brought up, how my life has been and how much I want to spend eternity with God and Joe helped me to stay on the path for which I am grateful.

*From Louise:*
I don't think there is any one thing that helps me in my grief. In my heart I know that Jerry is in heaven or in Paradise with Jesus now. Studying, praying, and worshipping makes me feel closer to him. I have made a point of reading scripture or devotionals every day and have spent

many, many days of praying and crying with God. I have felt a peace about Jerry's passing that I know was due to the many prayers offered for my benefit. Without the love of God and hope of a life in heaven my grief would be unbearable. Yes, the pandemic has been stressful in that we were unable to see our friends, but with modern technology, we have been able to text, talk, and even Face-Time several times. It has also been great that we have had daily devotions and we could attend church via the internet.

*From Elaine:*
I think two things that helped make being a widow easier, happened before the death of a spouse, at least for me. First, I was raised by two fine Christian parents. They raised me, by example, to be independent, happy, have close friends and attend church every time the doors were opened. As an adult I was able to enjoy teaching 40 years, be financially respon-

sible, make close Christians friends and attend church regularly.

I also think it is easier for most women to adjust to losing a spouse than it is for most men. Because women usually have the duties of cooking, cleaning, taking care of the family and often handling the finances, they can continue with daily routines.

Another thing with having close Christian friends, we feel comfortable going shopping out to eat, going to the movie, etc. with one or a group of friends. Men don't go out together as often, although several men from our congregation do play dominoes and visit the sick which is great.

Primetimers has been a very good program helping get close to people, and Ladies Bible Class has helped study the scriptures and learn about some of the new ladies.

***From Johnny:***

1. Short prayer as you get up. "Thanks for the rest last evening."

2. Short prayer as you go to bed. "Thanks for being with me this day."

3. Take time for bible study and reading. (I do it to start the day)

4. "Big prayer" for the church, others, family, and yourself.

5. I took an "enrichment" class at the junior college. (web design) to be sure and fill the day.

6. Use the "find a friend" function on the cell so kids can see where you are all the time.

7. A child visits with you at the end of each day.

8. Stay active in church.

***From Janelle:***

It seems almost expected that our faith will stumble when grief takes over. For

some people, maybe most, I can understand the heaviness of grief can certainly
test our faith. It can become easy to
blame or lose sight of Him. Sometimes, I
suppose, remaining faithful to God
seems to be in opposition to grief and
difficult situations in life. But I don't
think it needs to be that way.

For me, although I had never doubted
my faith, at this time in my life it also be-
came a choice. I was a young widow with
three children still at home and I was
working full time. The closest family was
an hour and a half away, and although
very supportive, were not available daily.
Oddly, and disappointingly, relationships
with many of our church friends we had
known as couples changed with my new
single status. God was the only source on
which I felt I could depend. There were
many talks with Him about my new life. I
felt an overwhelming responsibility to my
children to continue to make God a pri-
ority. My faith is what kept the rest of me

strong. Every situation is different. Every personality is different. Timings in life are different. People will react in different ways. It is not an easy road to walk. But if we focus on our walk with God first, grief and the responsibilities of life will become less of a struggle.

*From Martha:*
There are several things that have helped me to remain faithful to my Lord since losing Leon. First, I would say is my resolve to stay faithful to God throughout my life in all circumstances. Although it is hard to understand the reasons why God allowed this to happen, I do believe that God knows what was best for Leon and for me. God's word has encouraged and helped me so much to

remain faithful and to fully trust in Him to be with me. My faith is strengthened when I pour out my heart to my Father, telling Him about my feelings of sorrow, hurting, and loss, and asking Him to help me get through the difficult times. Another help to me was the example that I saw in my mother as her faith in God remained ever strong, even when she lost 3 sons in 5 years. These 2 short phrases have also helped:

> *Faith doesn't give us the answers,*
> *Faith allows us to live without the answers.*

> *God doesn't give us what we can handle,*
> *God helps us handle what we are given.*

 ### *From Bob*

The passage of scripture in II Corinthians 1:3-4 has become profound and foundational for me as I strive to live the remainder of my life here on this earth, following the loss of my dear wife, Diane.

I believe that my Heavenly Father gives me Comfort in several ways:

1. Through His Word, and the Promises contained therein.

2. Through the precious avenue of Prayer, in knowing that He is my Heavenly Father; and that as such, He loves me, He listens to my prayers, He answers my prayers, He wants only the very best for me, and He knows what is best for me. I frequently spend very lengthy periods of time, while in solitude, in my prayers of praise, thanksgiving, and requests to my Heavenly Father.

3. Through His Holy Spirit, who comforts in ways that I don't even know; although I do know that He intervenes on my behalf in my prayers to my Father.

4. Through my Family, Friends, and Fellow Christians.

5. Through the absolute Confidence that I have in Knowing that Diane is now Resting peacefully in the Presence of God and His Son, my Mother, and other fel-

low Christians who have gone on before me. Also, Knowing that Diane is no longer Suffering from, and having to deal with that terrible disease of Cancer.

6. Through the absolute Confidence in knowing that, even in spite of my many weaknesses and shortcomings, through the Grace and Mercy of my Heavenly Father, along with the cleansing Blood of His Son, I will Also one day Inherit Eternal Life; and then be Reunited with Diane, my mother, and other fellow Christians to spend Eternity together in the presence of God and His Son.

As a Recipient of this Comfort that my Heavenly Father gives to me, I am better equipped, and blessed to endeavor to Share and to pass along to others, that same Comfort that I have been Given.

 *From Lynda:*
I think the thing that helped me the most was my faithful to the Lord Christian

friends, many of whom had lost their spouses. They surrounded me with love and made sure I stayed busy. At least once a week, we met for lunch and a movie. We discussed many things, including my feelings of loss. They let me talk when I needed it and we laughed a lot about other things when I needed a laugh. I didn't feel so alone and knew I could call on any of them at any time.

*From Marilyn:*
I've never considered my faithfulness to God to be dependent on my circumstances, neither the loss of our child, nor the loss of my husband, nor the loss of our house by fire, etc. etc. I don't believe God caused these incidences to happen to me. Of course, I observed from my early childhood, that death was a part of life, and how my family dealt with this fact influenced me, probably more than I realize.

No matter where I am or what I'm doing, I almost always have a hymn in my mind, from awakening until bedtime. God and His Word are always available, anytime, anywhere, under any circumstances.

*From Dale:*
My wife, Sharon, had many physical problems and suffered greatly the last few years of her life. She never complained but would often say, "I can't wait until I get my new body!" After she passed away, I found great solace in the fact that she was no longer in pain and the next time I saw her she would have her new body!

*From Linda:*
Coming home to an "empty" house was hard for me—especially at first. I've had to re-focus and remind myself that I am not alone. God is with me to protect, guide and comfort me at all times.

*From Vickie:*
God blessed me with my sweet husband for 40 years and we were married for 34-1/2 of them. My husband passed away suddenly, and at that second, God was with me in comfort and guidance. He held me up when I could not stand. He surrounded me and my daughter with love by sending His people – my church family. They loved me, fed me, encouraged me, hugged me, spent precious time with me, cried with me, and laughed with me. Our preacher (and friend) got me and my family to the funeral home when I did not know what to do. Our Elders came to visit and asked if I needed anything. They were prepared to help in any way. I learned that God comforts us through His people. God shielded me with every wave of grief that came along, and I am so blessed to be His child through Christ.

Two weeks after my husband's passing friends took me out of town just to get away for a week and everywhere we went I saw this part of Psalm 46:10, "Be still and know that I am God." I literally saw that every day. And so, I bought a souvenir with that on it and God's word truly did help when I was still and turned things over to Him – the Great Comforter.

There are so many other Bible verses that are comforting, but these are the 3 that I took to heart as personal blessings for my grief journey. God has made this journey easier as time goes on and I am thankful for all His blessings that continue to help me through this life. The blessing of my church family has meant so much to me.

Getting back to church the next Sunday and sitting where we normally sat felt comforting to me. I recommend getting back to church as soon as you can. You will never get over it, you just have to get through it. With God's help you will. You cannot do it alone.

**From Sharon:**
I kept the faith because I want to be with God, and I want to see Lamar and other loved ones that have gone on before me.

I never wanted to live by myself and I still don't want to but who wants to marry a disabled woman and have to help her? it is a struggle and then to not have someone to talk to when something funny happens and you want to share it but can't. Or if you want to have someone to eat ice cream with you at night, there is no one there. No one there to share small talk with as you well know.

**From Robert:**
I'm fairly new to this "club," and wish I wasn't, as you know, and I'm sure you wish too. But here we are. It's so hard right now, and I feel like I'm drowning in sorrow. The one thing that keeps me going is knowing this is what Karen would want me to do. Everywhere we have been, it has been a joint ministry you

might say. When we would go to a new work, we prayed about it, talked about it, and decided on it together, along with if it was best for the kids. She had her work in the congregation, usually teaching the kiddos in Bible class, but going with me to the hospital, Bible studies, everything she could participate in. She defended me and supported me when members unfairly attacked. We were a team. So, I know she would be telling me not to sit around feeling sorry for myself, but to get back in it. Being able to write lessons, classes, and sermons, is a positive thing that keeps my mind occupied a lot of the time, but obviously not all the time. I feel like I'm pleasing God and honoring her life by preaching the word each week. So, I sit where we always sat, knowing she would still be there if she were here. I draw strength from things like that. For her to be in Paradise, I must work while it's still day to be with her again someday.

It's so tough thinking about her not being here, and that the life we had together here is over, and that eternity will be radically different. But she supported me so much, and gave up so much, for me to do this, it would be a dishonor not to continue the work she invested her very being in. And I can say this. She had multiple health issues, bad asthma being one. She knew the risk of getting out, knowing COVID and her lungs would be at odds. But she never missed an assembly the whole time, until we got it. She attended and did all she could the whole time. When I hear of people that can go anywhere and everywhere but the assembly, I remember her willingness to put God first in everything. I will honor that by doing the same in my work in His kingdom. That's what gets me up every day and keeps me going.

*"Sometimes our hearts,*
*Know sorrow and pain,*
*Days without sunshine,*

*Days filled with rain.*
*But we do not grieve,*
*without having hope,*
*In the promises of Jesus,*
*with these we will cope."*

(Written by Robert Johnson in memory of Karen Johnson.)

# RESOURCES

### *Ron & Don Williams*

These twin brothers have been dear friends for most of my life. They have helped thousands through their books, workshops, and other resources. I can't recommend them enough. You can find out more on their website. https://rondonbooks.com/ Ron & Don can also help you start a Grief Support Group in your home congregation.

### *Widowhood Workshop*

Dean Miller lost his wife several years ago and begin encouraging others who have lost a spouse. He wrote a wonderful book entitled, "When the End Comes." You can find the book, along with several additional helps, and learn more about the workshops on his website. www.widowhoodworkshop.com

### *Stephen Ministries*

There are a number of great resources found on this website. https://www.stephenministries.org/default.cfm

## *Books*

*Don't Take My Grief Away: What to Do When You Lose a Loved One.* (Doug Manning)

*Good Grief.* (Granger E. Westberg)

If I can ever be of help to you please feel free to reach out to me at: *jeffajenkins@gmail.com*

# ADDITIONAL TITLES FROM TJI

*The Living Word: Sermons of Jerry A. Jenkins*

*Thoughts from the Mound*
*More Thoughts from the Mound*
*All I Ever Wanted to Do Was Preach*
*I Hope You Have to Pinch Yourself*

*The Preacher as Counselor*

*Don't Quit on a Monday*
*Don't Quit on a Tuesday*
*Don't Quit on a Wednesday*
*Don't Quit on a Thursday*
*Don't Quit on a Friday*

*Five Secrets and a Decision*
*Centered: Marking Your Map in a Muddled World*
*On Moving Well: The Scoop-Meister's Thoughts on Ministry Transitions*
*Praying Always: Prayers for Preachers (gift book for ministers)*
*Now What? Surviving a Forced Termination*

*A Minister's Heart*
*A Youth Minister's Heart*
*A Mother's Heart*
*A Father's Heart*

*Immerse: A Simple Look at Baptism*

To order, visit **thejenkinsinstitute.com/shop**

# ADDITIONAL TITLES FROM TJI

To order, visit **thejenkinsinstitute.com/shop**

Made in the USA
Coppell, TX
05 December 2023

25324411R00052